Jump Rope Time

by Kana Riley
illustrated by Debbie Tilley

Scott Foresman

Editorial Offices: Glenview, Illinois • New York, New York
Sales Offices: Reading, Massachusetts • Duluth, Georgia
Glenview, Illinois • Carrollton, Texas • Menlo Park, California

Who can jump rope?

Jan can.

She is good at it.

Look at Jan go!

Tim can.

He is good at it too.

But I am not.

I turn the rope.

I jump.

I miss.

I turn the rope.

I jump.

I miss.

I jump some more.

I miss some more!

So I do it one more time.

I turn the rope.

I jump.

I turn.

I jump.

I turn.

I jump!

Now who can jump rope?

Tim can.
Jan can.

And I can too!
Now I can jump rope.

I do it all the time.